AlphaSCAMPS™
Big Words Adventure

Written and Illustrated by
JANIS RICHMAN

GLOSSARY INCLUDED

AlphaScamps Big Words Adventure
Copyright © 2023 by Janis Richman
Written and Illustrated by Janis Richman

All rights reserved. No part of this book may be reproduced or transmitted in any form or by any means without written permission from the publisher and author.

Additional copies may be ordered from the publisher for educational, business, promotional or premium use. For information, contact ALIVE Book Publishing at:
alivebookpublishing.com

ISBN 13
978-1-63132-206-8 Paperback
978-1-63132-213-6 Hardcover

Library of Congress Control Number: 2023914918
Library of Congress Cataloging-in-Publication Data is available upon request.

First Edition

Published in the United States of America by ALIVE Book Publishing and ALIVE Publishing Group, imprints of Advanced Publishing LLC
3200 A Danville Blvd., Suite 204, Alamo, California 94507
alivebookpublishing.com

PRINTED IN THE UNITED STATES OF AMERICA

10 9 8 7 6 5 4 3 2 1

How to use this book

Help kids find the BIG WORDS in each rhyming story.

Use the glossary included to stretch their vocabulary.

Acknowledgments

I give thanks to the infinite intelligence that drew together with great synchronicity all the wonderful people who supported me in making this book come to life. This is really OUR book.

Getting back to my illustration roots may never have happened had it not been for David Bittorf. David, I am so grateful for your superb digital art classes and our wonderful brainstorming sessions. You were there for the birth of the book and guided me all the way through to its completion. Thank you!

It was a challenge to figure out how to lay out all the images and content so the book flowed easily—until I met Deborah Perdue. Not only is she my favorite production person, but she is a spiritual sister in every way. Deborah, I am so thankful for your guidance and patience as the book kept morphing into its final format.

Christine Atkins, what would I have done without your vast knowledge and experience in how children learn? Thank you for ensuring that I was speaking to the widest audience including children of all skills and abilities. Your inclusivity and learning insights were invaluable.

Deep gratitude to my Bindi sisters, Mahnaz Rastakhiz, Suzanne Albertson, and Farzana Khan. Thank you for always being there to support and cheer me on, and for giving me feedback that moved me forward. How good it is to have best friends with infinite patience and great aesthetics!

Thank you dear fellow writers and illustrators from my monthly mastermind group. Your support, feedback, and willingness to share your expertise have made all the difference!

So many thanks to my family and friends who tirelessly listened to my stream-of-consciousness rhyming and who talked me off the ledge when I couldn't write one more definition. So many of your recommendations have made their way into this book. As you read the book, I can hear you saying, "Hey, that was my idea!"

And, of course, sincere thanks to Eric Johnson and the Alive Publishing team. Thanks, Eric, for seeing the potential of the AlphaScamps and Scampanions vision. I am so grateful to work with people who really "got me," understood what I was trying to do, and then gave me everything I needed to do it.

This book is dedicated to my sister Linda, who was an incredible artist, tai chi master and had the strongest will of anyone I have ever known. I would have chosen her as a best friend had she not already been my sister. While Linda was not here to collaborate with me, I always felt her artistic presence.

For all this and so much more, I give thanks.

The AlphaScamps™ are great kids just like you,

doing what all great kids love to do.

Meet them on the letter that starts their first name.

You too can be an AlphaScamp™
when your letter is the same!

Meet the
SCAMPANIONS

Froggy Kitty Shaggy

Fishy Octi Peri Yorki

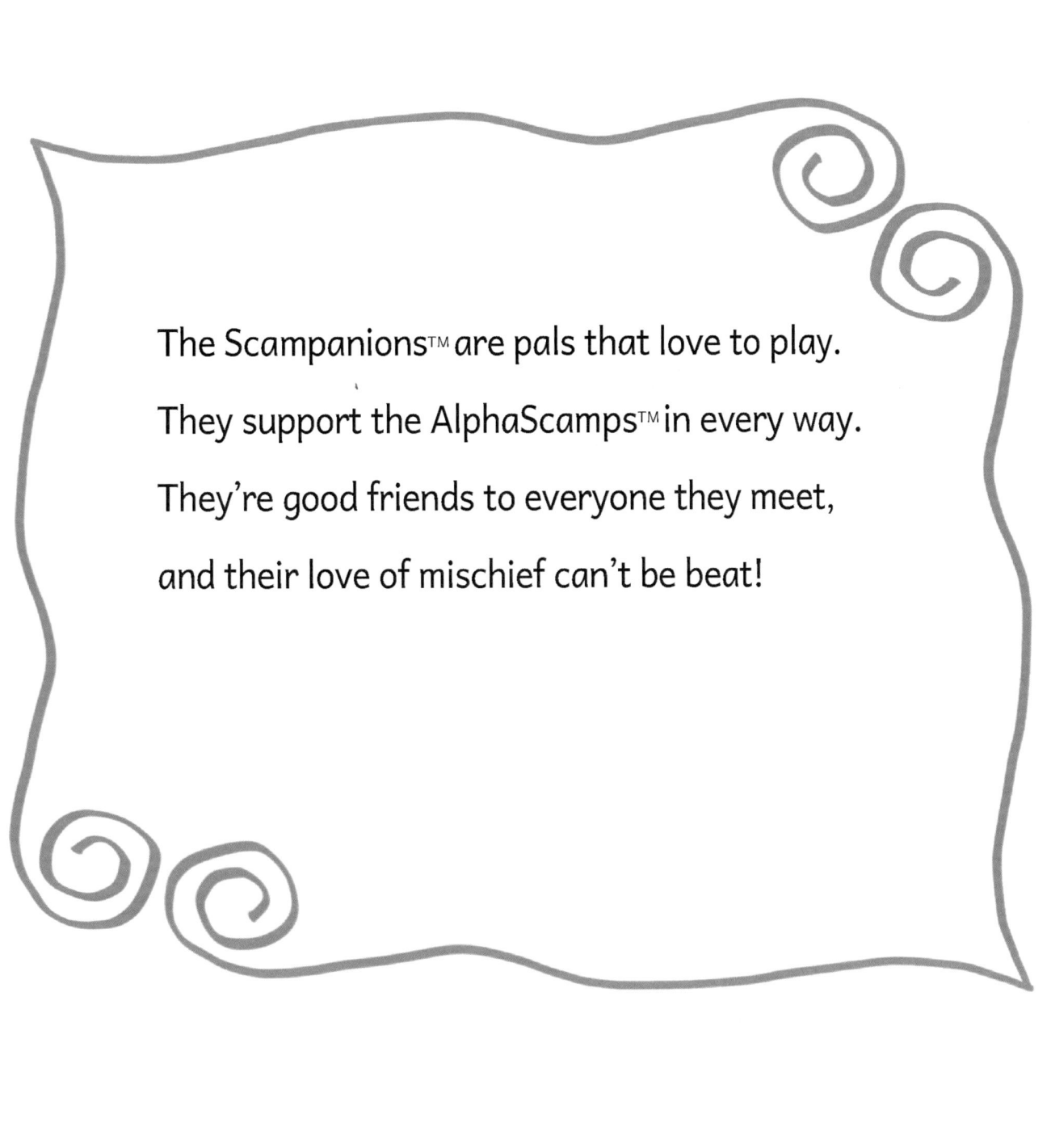

The Scampanions™ are pals that love to play.

They support the AlphaScamps™ in every way.

They're good friends to everyone they meet,

and their love of mischief can't be beat!

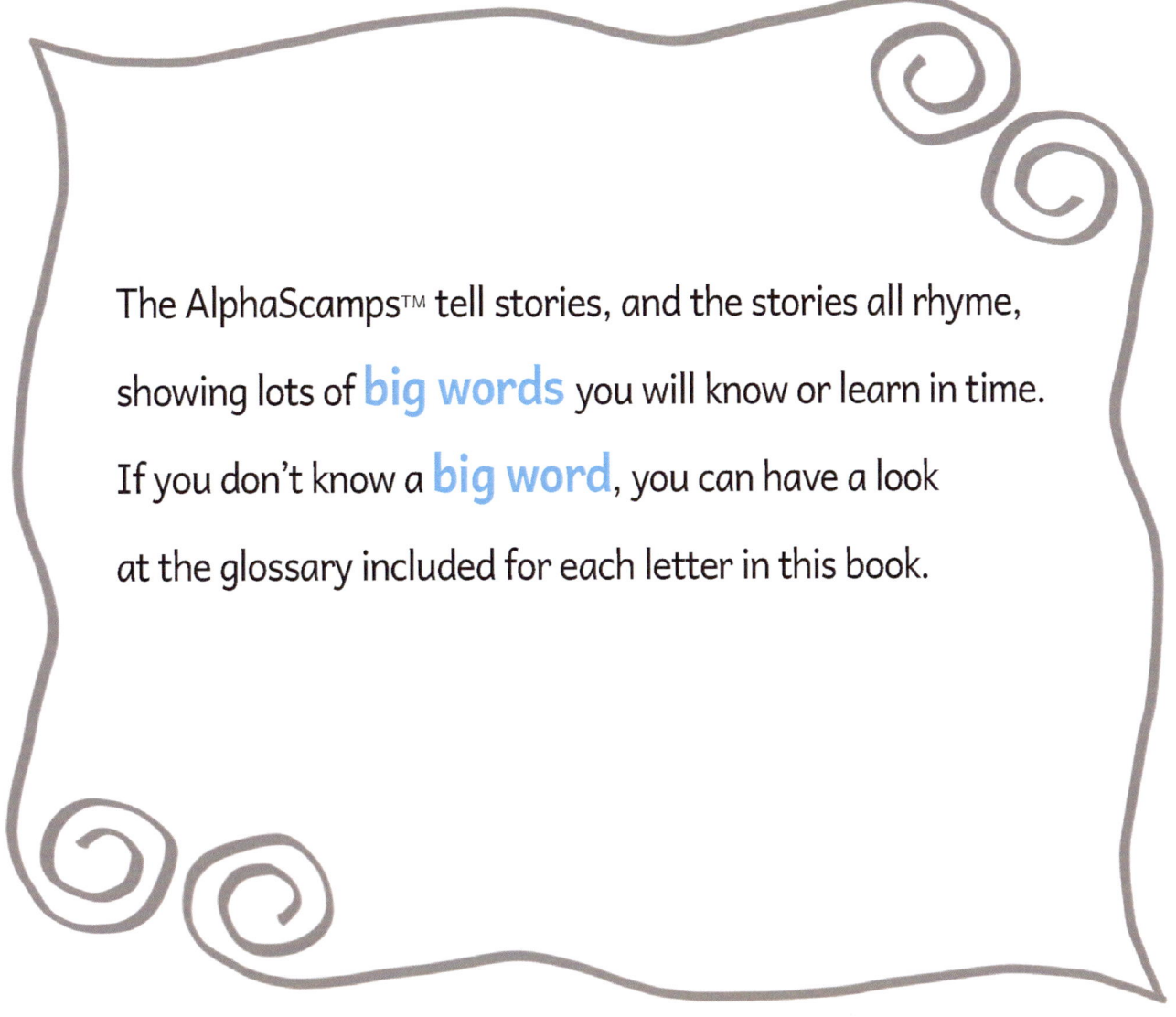

The AlphaScamps™ tell stories, and the stories all rhyme, showing lots of **big words** you will know or learn in time. If you don't know a **big word**, you can have a look at the glossary included for each letter in this book.

BIG WORD GLOSSARY

Discover what the BIG WORDS mean or refresh what you already know. Because these definitions have a lot of action, feeling and sound, we call them "Definactions."

Adam loves skateboarding all around town.

He does **amazing antics** in the air and the ground.

Froggy is always asking to skate along,

and they **appreciate** sharing an **awesome** song.

A

amazing	[*adjective*] When something really surprises us and is unexpected and gives us pleasure, we say it's amazing...WOW!
antic	[*noun*] Antics are wild and funny actions or playful tricks, just like when Adam flips his skateboard in the air.
appreciate	[*verb*] When we appreciate someone or something, we are very grateful and admire who or what they are.
awesome	[*adjective*] Something awesome is super-good. When you think a person is awesome, you are filled with wonder and respect.

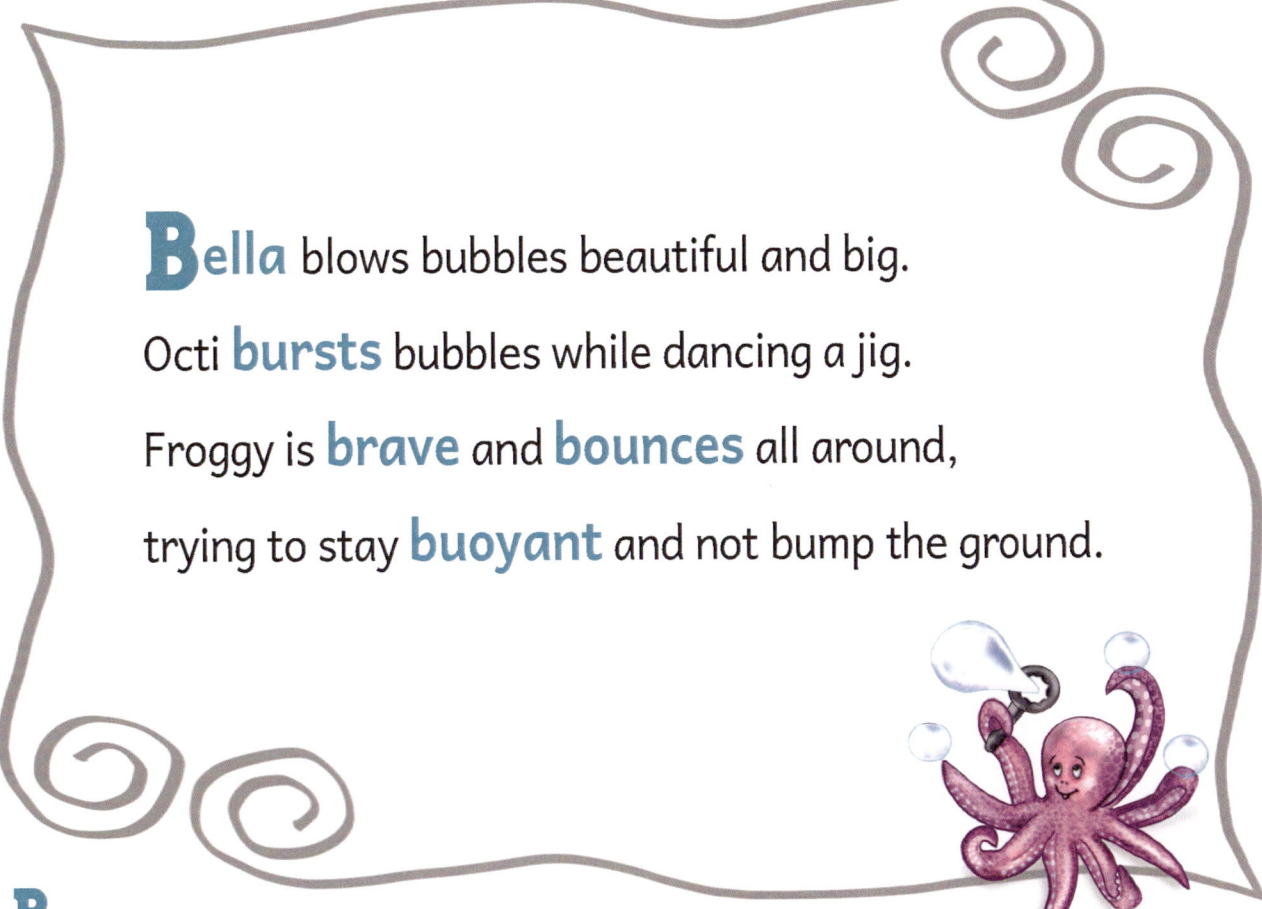

Bella blows bubbles beautiful and big.

Octi **bursts** bubbles while dancing a jig.

Froggy is **brave** and **bounces** all around,

trying to stay **buoyant** and not bump the ground.

B

bounce	[*verb*] When we bounce, we spring right back up after hitting something. BOING!
brave	[*adjective*] When we are brave, we may be afraid, but we don't let it stop us; we are courageous.
buoyant	[*adjective*] When someone or something is floating on a liquid or air they are buoyant. It can also mean cheerful or lighthearted.
burst	[*verb*] When something bursts, it explodes suddenly. POP!!

Casey and Yorki are **comfy** and cuddly.

Teddy Bear touches their cheeks lovingly.

They love being **cozy** and want to **commune**,

and Peri is **cheerful** while **caressing** the moon.

caress	[*noun*] When we want to hug something we love but don't want to squish it, we give it a gentle caress — a soft squeeze.
cheerful	[*adjective*] When we are doing something we love, it makes us smile and laugh — it makes us cheerful.
comfy	[*adjective*] When we are snuggled and cuddled in our favorite blanket, it makes us feel comfy.
commune	[*verb*] When we communicate with someone with great love and trust, we are communing with them.
cozy	[*adjective*] Cozy is when we are warm and snug in a comfortable way.

David is **drenched** and Octi is dripping.

Fishy throws **droplets** and then goes **dipping**.

Soon they'll get **doused** as they look in one direction,

while waves sneak up without their **detection**.

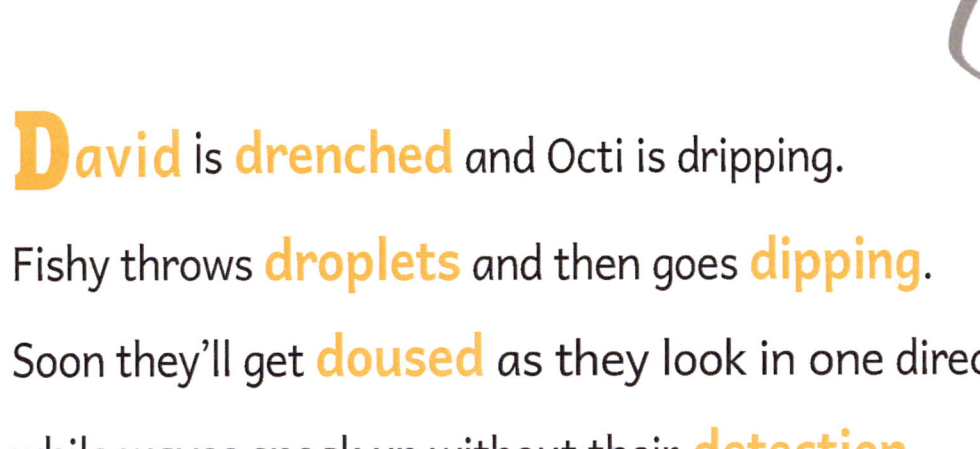

D

detection	[*noun*] Detection is noticing something. When someone sneaks by us and we don't notice, we say they passed us without detection.
dipping	[*verb*] When we are quickly putting something into a liquid and then pulling it out, we are dipping it.
douse	[*verb*] When we splash or throw lots of water at everyone, we are dousing them.
drenched	[*adjective*] What happens when we get caught in the heavy rain with no umbrella — we get drenched.
droplets	[*noun*] Droplets are small water drops, like when a wet dog shakes off water, we get splashed with droplets.

Everett **exercises** at the gym every week.

Each workout is easy, **engaging** and unique.

Froggy and Octi want to learn the **equipment**,

and they all get **excited** to learn something different.

engaging	[*verb*]	When we like something and want to experience more of it, we call it engaging.
equipment	[*noun*]	Things that are made or used for a particular activity are called equipment.
excited	[*adjective*]	We are excited when our feelings get all stirred up, like when we can't wait to try something new.
exercise	[*noun*]	Activities we do to help keep our body or mind strong are called exercises, like when Octi bounces on the trampoline.

Franky and friends love a painting fight.

They fling paint and watch the flecks in flight.

Fishy's face was hiding in all of the flurry.

They're ready to finish the fence in a hurry.

F

fleck	[*noun*] Tiny patches of light or color, like the flecks of purple paint on Franky's sneakers.
flight	[*noun*] Flight means something moving through space, like Franky tossing the paint in the air.
fling	[*verb*] When we need to throw a ball as hard as we can, we fling it with force.
flurry	[*noun*] When leaves twist and twirl in the wind, we call that a flurry of leaves.

Grace gathers together a musical group.

Kitty and Peri are grateful to sing with this troupe.

Froggy plays the guitar and does it with glee.

Grabbing ears is a must when they all sing off-key.

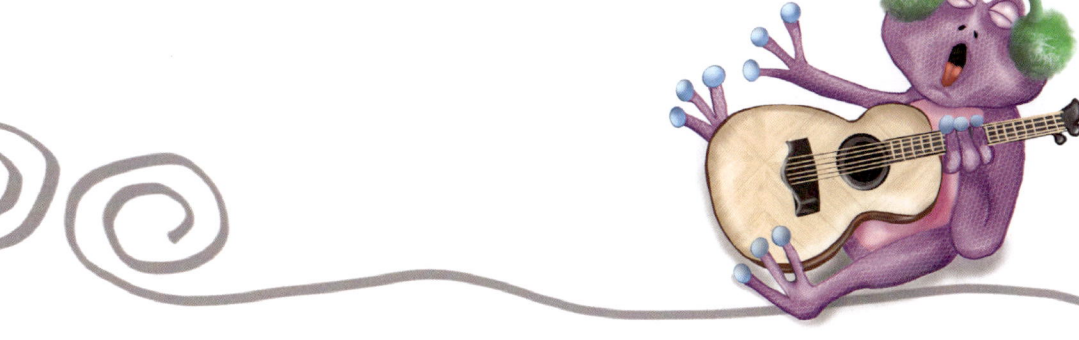

G

gather	[*verb*] When we bring together people or things into one place, we gather them.
glee	[*noun*] We are filled with glee when we have a feeling of delight or joy. Hooray!
grabbing	[*verb*] When we snatch something quickly, like grabbing an apple from the tree when we are hungry.
grateful	[*adjective*] When we are grateful, we feel thankful for all the kindness and goodness we receive.

H

harmony [*noun*] Harmony is a pleasing arrangement of people, music or things. When we experience harmony, we feel peaceful.

howling [*adjective*] Crying out loudly and with all your might is called howling, like when Shaggy howls at a firetruck that's going by.

humming [*verb*] When we hear a low, steady, continuous sound, we say it is humming. Peri likes to imitate the sound of bees by humming.

Isabella **investigates** the ants and bees.

They're the most **intelligent** insects you ever will see.

Shaggy and Kitty like to **inquire** around

to get **information** the ants share from the ground.

I

information	[*noun*] When we get facts from someone or something, we get information, like watching ants to see how they work together.
inquire	[*verb*] We inquire when we ask a question in order to receive an answer.
intelligent	[*adjective*] Intelligent means having a great ability to understand something, like bees who communicate in amazing ways.
investigate	[*verb*] When we want information, we look at things carefully and closely to learn the facts — that's called investigating.

Jackson loves **juggling**; it gives him great joy.

Balls **jumping** in the air are his pals' favorite toy.

They are **joyful** when juggling — with smiles all around.

The balls all may **jiggle**, but stay off the ground.

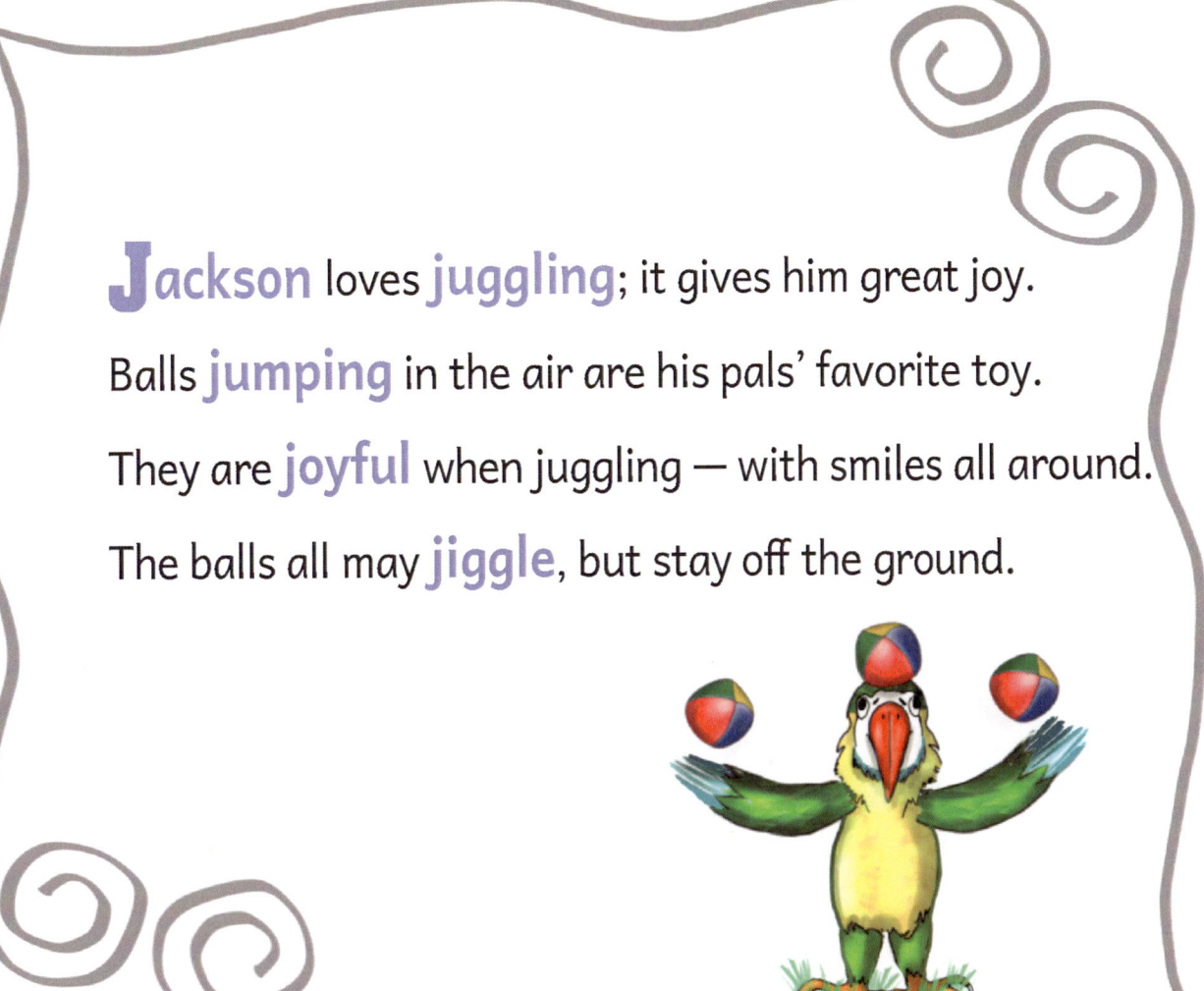

J

jiggle	[verb] When something jiggles, it move up and down and back and forth — just like jello!
joyful	[noun] When we feel happy all over and want to smile, we are feeling joyful.
juggle	[verb] If we can keep something in the air while tossing and catching it, we can juggle.
jumping	[verb] When something leaps into the air, it is jumping, like when we see a cat jump over a fence.

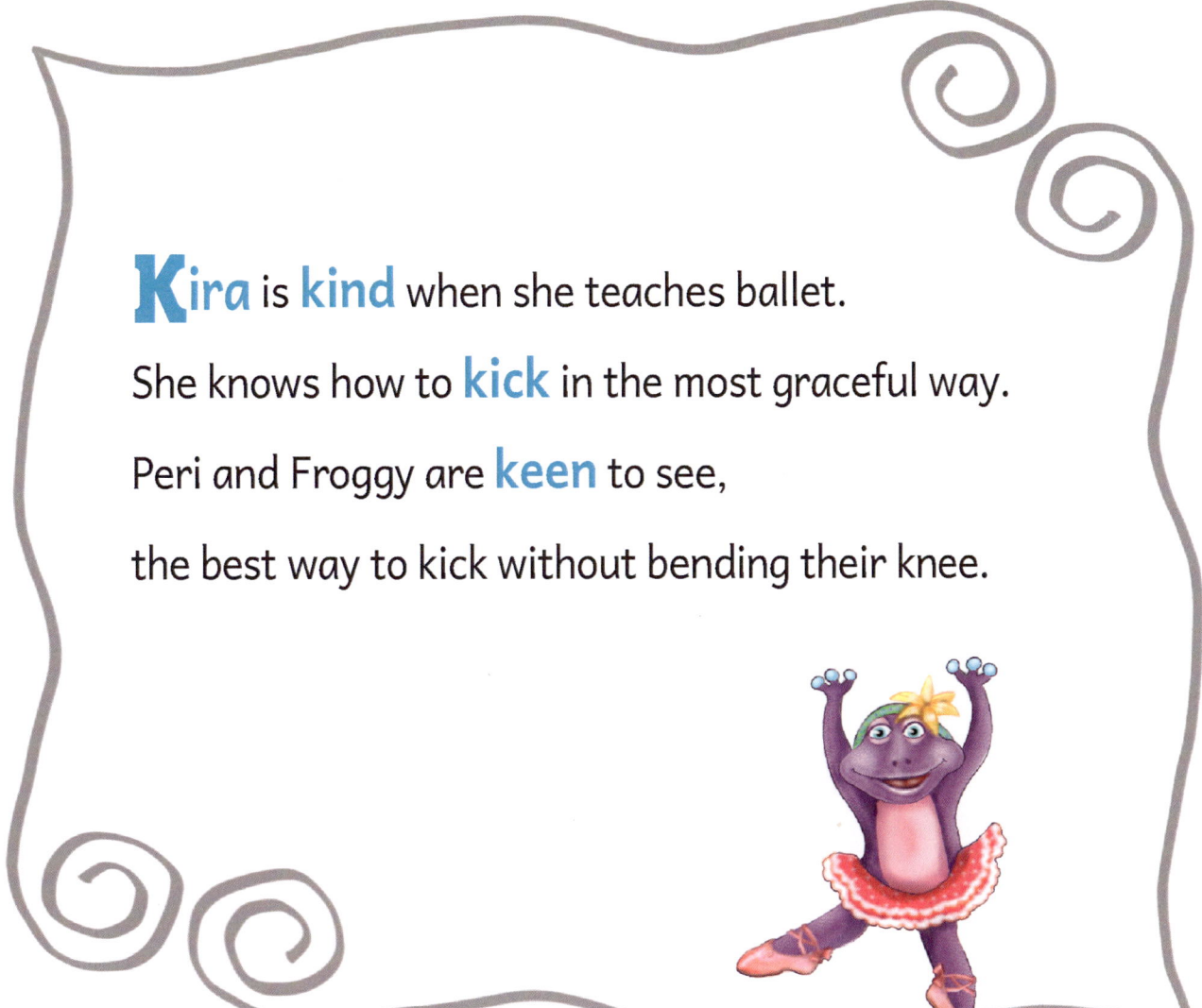

Kira is **kind** when she teaches ballet.

She knows how to **kick** in the most graceful way.

Peri and Froggy are **keen** to see,

the best way to kick without bending their knee.

K

keen   [*adjective*] When we are excited and really want to do something, we can say we are keen to do it.

kick   [*verb*] A dance move where we strike our foot in the air — usually in front, behind or to the side of the other leg. Try it!

kind   [*adjective*] When someone is helpful or friendly or good, we say they are kind.

Leah hangs her **laundry** in the sunshine.

She **lifts** and **leans** to reach the clothesline.

Octi **lends** many hands to **lighten** the **loads**,

while Kitty lies **lurking** in **linens** and clothes.

L

laundry	[*noun*] Laundry can be all kinds of things that are cleaned by washing.
lean	[*verb*] Leaning is bending in a certain direction, like when we lean towards someone to hear them whisper.
lend	[*verb*] We lend a hand when we offer to provide help to someone.
lift	[*verb*] When we raise something upward, we lift it.
lighten	[*verb*] When we reduce the weight of something, we lighten it, like making the laundry basket lighter by getting Kitty to jump out!
linen	[*noun*] Linen is a cloth made from a special plant called flax.
load	[*noun*] A load is a bundle of stuff we have to carry, like our school books!

Maxie is living a *marvelous* dream.

All the Scampanions have just *made* the team.

They dribble and *maneuver* across the floor.

Kitty's a *master* at dunking with one paw.

M

made	[*verb*] When we achieve something or we get chosen for a purpose, we can say that we have made it! Hurrah!
maneuver	[*verb*] We maneuver when we move from one place to another using a plan, like zig-zagging the ball across the floor.
marvelous	[*adjective*] We say something is marvelous when it gives us wonder or amazement.
master	[*verb*] We are masters at something when we become an expert at it.

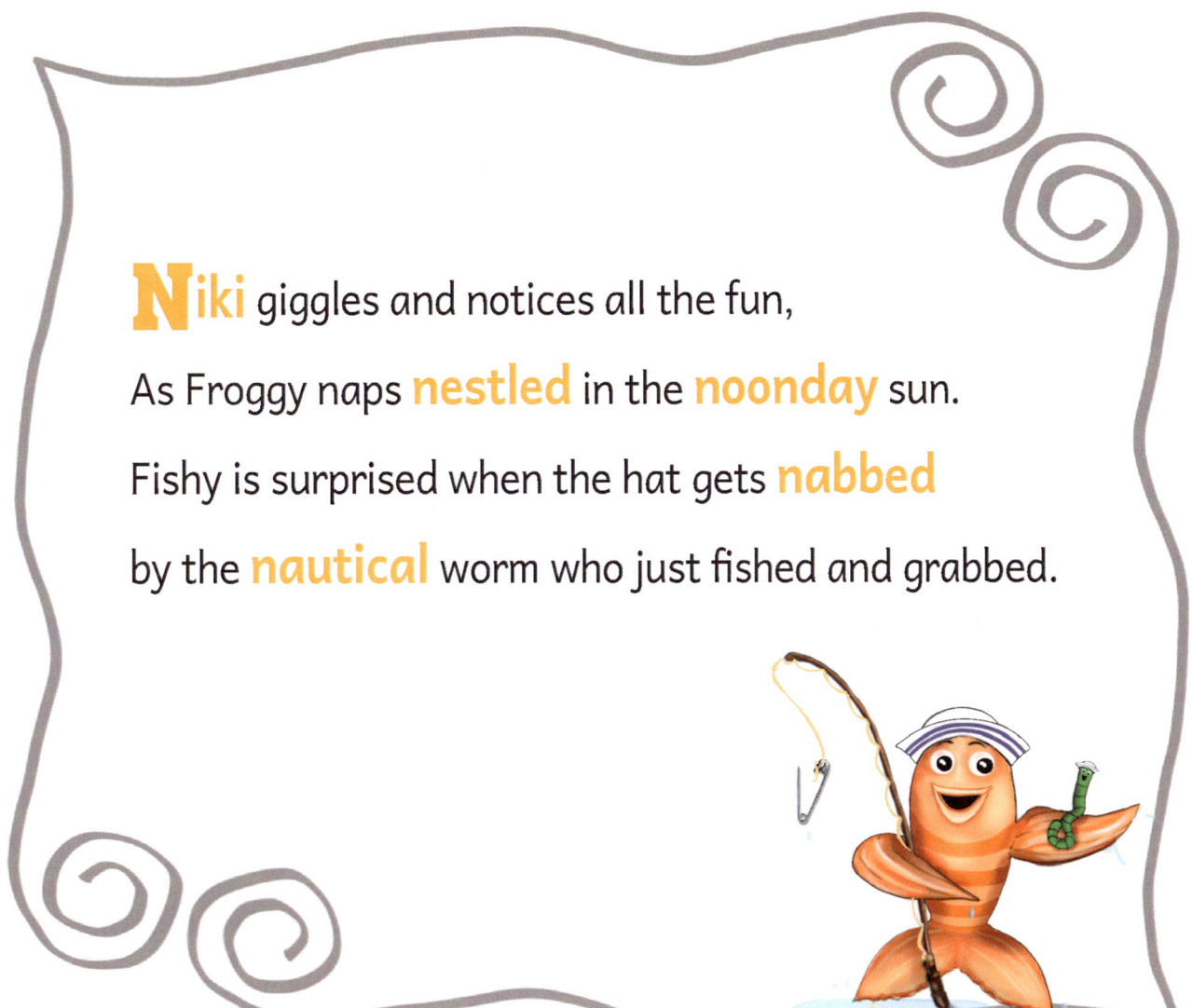

Niki giggles and notices all the fun,

As Froggy naps **nestled** in the **noonday** sun.

Fishy is surprised when the hat gets **nabbed**

by the **nautical** worm who just fished and grabbed.

N

nab [*verb*] When we grab something from someone, we are nabbing it.

nautical [*adjective*] Anything that has to do with the sea, sailing, or sailors is called nautical.

nestle [*verb*] When we lie close or curled up next to something or someone, we say we are nestled.

noonday [*adjective*] Noonday is another way of saying 12 Noon.

Olivia loves playing outside with others.

Froggy's found an **oasis** to give shade and cover.

When the sun **overhead** is hot as an oven,

Octi cools in water **obtained** from the ocean.

O

oasis	[*noun*]	An oasis is a place in the desert where plants can grow.
obtain	[*verb*]	Obtain is a fancy way to say get or receive.
overhead	[*adverb*]	Something or someone is overhead if it is located right above our head, and it doesn't matter how far up it is.

Pamela plays in the water without using a boat.

Her **plastic platypus** always keeps her afloat.

When walking on the beach or playing inside,

Fishy **perches** on the tube and goes for a ride.

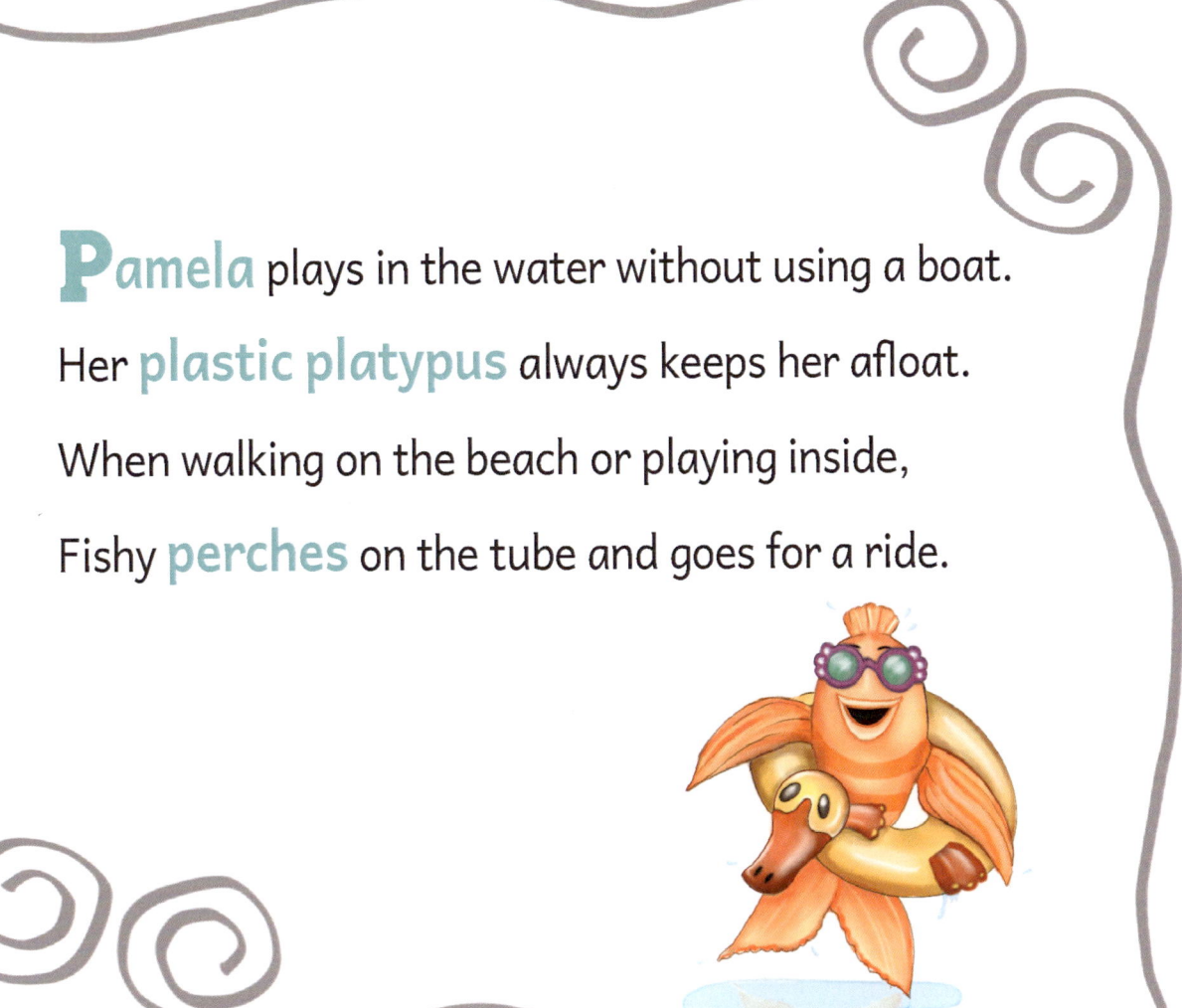

P

perch	[*verb*] We perch when we come to rest on something — even a swimming tube! Birds like to perch on telephone wires.
plastic	[*noun*] Plastic is made from chemicals that can be molded into different forms when soft and hardens into all kinds of shapes.
platypus	[*noun*] Platypuses are mammals with wide bills, long, flat tails, and webbed feet for swimming. They live in Australia.

Quincy and Kitty have a **quiz** that is easy.

But all quizzes seem to make them both **queasy**.

So they take a **quiet** breath, which always calms,

and **quickly** ace their quizzes without any **qualms**.

Q

qualm	[*noun*] When we are not sure we can or even should do something, we say we have qualms about doing it.
queasy	[*adjective*] That feeling when our tummy gets upset because of something we ate or sometimes when we are afraid of something.
quickly	[*adverb*] When we did something really fast and in a short time, we say we did it quickly.
quiet	[*adjective*] Quiet is when something or someone is not making a sound or noise.
quiz	[*verb*] A quiz is when we are asked questions to test what we know.

Robin relishes winter when she gets to skate,

She can see her reflection on the frozen lake.

Fishy rises from the ice and reveals a surprise!

Hats resemble each other, but are not the same size.

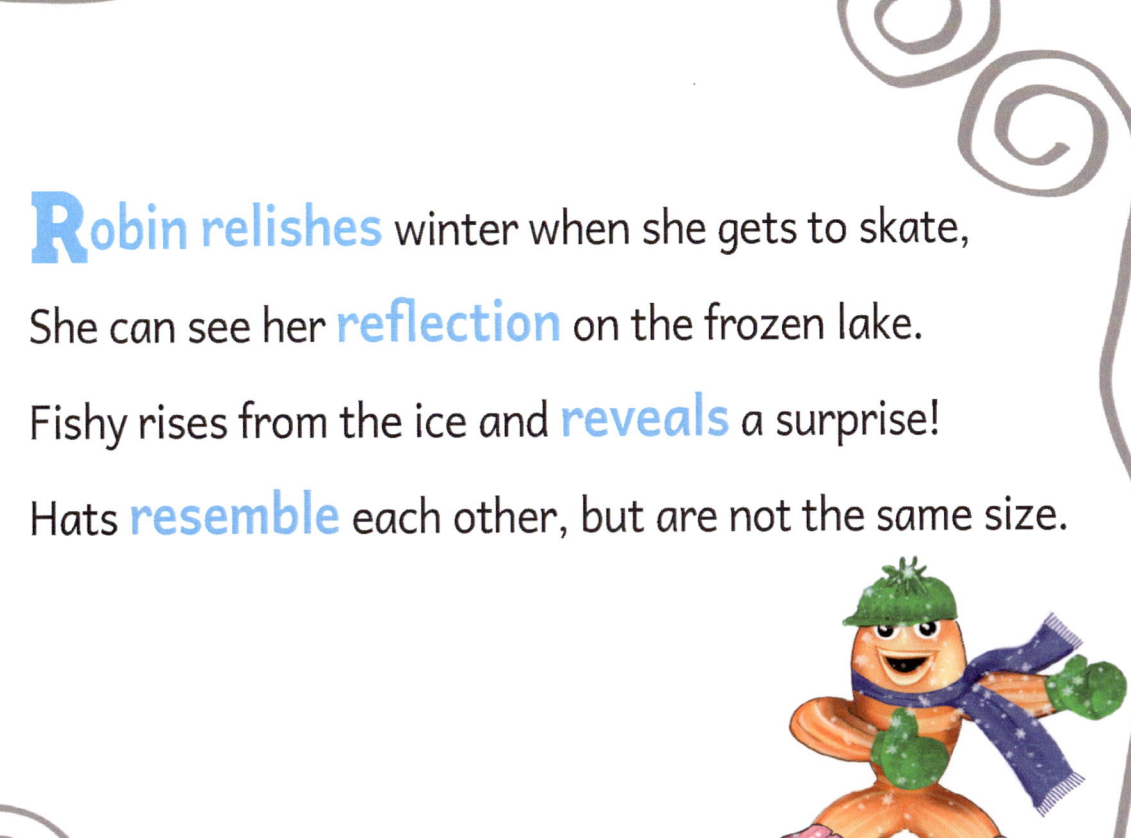

R

reflection   [*noun*] When something shines back at us, and we see that image, it is called a reflection, like looking in a mirror.

relish   [*noun*] When we get great enjoyment from something, we relish it.

resemble   [*verb*] Resemble is when something or someone is similar and looks alike, like twins or family members or even matching hats!

reveal   [*verb*] When something or someone is hidden and then shows up, it is revealed.

Sadie is drowsy and takes a short nap.

Yorki **snuggles** and **snoozes** in her soft lap.

Shaggy **snores** and **snorts** without a care,

which **startles** and awakens sleeping teddy bear.

s

snooze	[*verb*] We snooze when we take a nap or sleep for a short period of time.
snore	[*verb*] Snoring is that loud breathing and funny noise we sometimes hear when people sleep.
snort	[*verb*] We snort when we push air through our nose in a noisy way. Pigs and horses snort!
snuggle	[*verb*] We snuggle when we lie next to someone or something in a comfortable way.
startle	[*verb*] We are startled when we get surprised.

T

tease [*verb*] When we tease someone, we try to annoy them or get their attention, but we do it in a playful way.

topple [*verb*] Something swaying back and forth and falling down is called toppling.

toss [*verb*] When we toss something, we throw it gently — sometimes because we want to be sure the other person catches it.

trip [*noun*] Falling or stumbling is called tripping.

Ulli's **umpire uniform** is pink and green.

Scampanions were **underdogs** but are now a top team.

Octi in **unison** plays all positions and places.

Froggy's **ultimate** goal is to steal all the bases.

U

umpire	[*noun*] An umpire is the person who makes sure all the rules of a game are followed and that no one cheats.
underdog	[*noun*] An underdog is a person or team that is expected to lose a contest or game.
uniform	[*noun*] A uniform is a special suit of clothing that is worn by everyone in a group.
unison	[*noun*] When we do something in unison, we are doing it all at the same time.
ultimate	[*adjective*] The very best or final thing we hope to achieve.

Val plays **video** games when homework is done.

The Scampanions keep **vying**, but still haven't won.

They're always on the **verge** of winning a round,

but Val is **victorious**, even upside down.

verge	[*noun*] When we are just about to do something, we are on the verge of doing it.
victorious	[*adjective*] When we win at something, we are victorious. YAY!
video	[*noun*] Video games are games played on the computer.
vying	[*verb*] When we compete with another to win something, we are vying and want to be victorious.

Wendy started the garden with water and seeds.

Peri loves all the **wildflowers**, even the weeds.

The bees are their **workmates**, including the queen.

They all make a **whimsical** gardening team.

whimsical	[*adjective*] When we see something silly and amusing, we say it is whimsical.
wildflower	[*noun*] Wildflowers are plants that grow without any help from people, and can be very beautiful.
workmate	[*noun*] a workmate is a person who works in the same place as you.

Xavier gets **eXcited** whenever he skis.

He **eXplores** the mountains as he flies past the trees.

Yorki **eXclaims**, "*Please take me home,*

where it's warm, and I'll play with my toy **xylophone**."

X

excited   [*adjective*] We are excited when we have strong feelings about something or someone.

explores   [*verb*] When we look at something in a careful way to learn more about it, we explore it.

exclaims   [*verb*] We exclaim when we cry out or speak suddenly with strong feeling or delight.

xylophone   [*noun*] A xylophone is an instrument you play by hitting metal or wooden bars with small wooden hammers.

Yancy and Kitty do **yoga** at dawn.

The time is so early, it makes them both **yawn**.

Yet they do all positions, then lie on their tummy,

and **yearn** for a breakfast delicious and **yummy**.

Y

yawn	[*noun*] We yawn when we open our mouth, take a deep breath, and exhale loudly. We may be sleepy or bored.
yearn	[*verb*] That feeling we get when we really wish for something to happen, like eating pancakes for breakfast!
yoga	[*noun*] Yoga is a practice of physical and mental exercises that can help train our body and mind.
yummy	[*adjective*] Something that is very tasty and delicious.

Zoe goes **zipping** with **zest** and **zeal**.

Octi loves the way zig-zagging makes everyone feel.

As they both reach the **zenith** and look all around,

they raise up their arms and **zoom** their way down.

z

zeal	[*noun*] We feel zeal when we experience great enthusiasm for a person or something we are doing.
zenith	[*noun*] A zenith is the very highest point of something.
zest	[*noun*] When feeling zest, we are experiencing a sense of great pleasure or enjoyment.
zipping	[*verb*] Moving or acting with speed and energy is called zipping.
zoom	[*verb*] When we zoom, we are moving or traveling quickly, just like when Zoe and Octi ride the rollercoaster.

But wait, there's more!

AlphaSCAMPS™

You can order…

- A signed copy of the book
- Custom names in acrylic tiles
- Letter t-shirts, and more…

Go to: AlphaScamps.com

ABOOKS

ALIVE Book Publishing and ALIVE Publishing Group
are imprints of Advanced Publishing LLC,
3200 A Danville Blvd., Suite 204, Alamo, California 94507

Telephone: 925.837.7303
alivebookpublishing.com

www.ingramcontent.com/pod-product-compliance
Lightning Source LLC
Chambersburg PA
CBRC091451160426
43202CB00006B/21